American Essentials

EASIER COMPOSITIONS FOR PIANO

SELECTED AND EDITED BY LAWRENCE ROSEN

ED 3980

ISBN 0-7935-8632-1

G. SCHIRMER, Inc.

Distributed By
HAL•LEONARD CORPORATION
7777 W. BLUEMOUND RD. P.O. BOX 13819 MILWAUKEE, WI 53213

Copyright © 1998 by G. Schirmer, Inc. (ASCAP), New York, NY
International Copyright Secured.   All Rights Reserved.
Warning: Unauthorized reproduction of this publication is
prohibited by Federal law and subject to criminal prosecution.

PREFACE

Creating good music for the beginning or intermediate pianist has always been a challenge, even for the most gifted composers. Some of them have shown a special gift for producing short, original piano pieces of moderate scope and technical difficulty which, nonetheless, perfectly distill the musical and technical essence of their larger, more ambitious works for the keyboard. Bach did this (*Notebook of Anna Magdalena*, some of the *Inventions*), but Handel rarely did; Liszt (*Five Little Piano Pieces*, *Nuages Gris*), but not Chopin; Schumann (*Album for the Young*) but not Brahms; and Bartók (*Mikrokosmos*, *Album for the Young*) but not Stravinsky.

In this tradition, *American Essentials* offers a remarkably wide-ranging group of piano pieces by some of America's most celebrated composers. These pieces (with the exception of the Barber and Menotti selections) were all originally composed for the piano; they are not transcriptions or arrangements. They are designed to introduce the pianist in the earlier stages of technical and musical development to new techniques of composition and piano playing, ideally preparing and inspiring the student to further exploration of more challenging 20th century masterworks. Thus, they are useful not only in the pianistic development of the young student, but as a gateway to the many new musical approaches of recent decades.

The pieces are arranged in approximate order of technical difficulty. In some passages, the editor has put parentheses around notes that may be omitted, for those who are still unable to negotiate octaves and other technical difficulties.

—Lawrence Rosen

CONTENTS

Samuel Barber	*Under the Willow Tree* (from *Vanessa*)	2
David Diamond	from *Eight Piano Pieces*:	
	No. 1, *Pease-Porridge Hot*	4
	No. 2, *Jumping Jacks*	5
	No. 6, *Rock-a-Bye, Baby*	6
	No. 8, *Lullaby*	7
Morton Gould	from *10 for Deborah*:	
	Tango	8
	Wistful	10
	Drifting	11
	Loud and Soft	12
	Melody	15
	A Happy Ending	16
Edward MacDowell	*To a Wild Rose* (from *Woodland Sketches*)	18
Philip Glass	*Metamorphosis One*	20
	Metamorphosis Three	24
Robert Muczynski	from *Fables*:	
	No. 1	29
	No. 8	30
	No. 9	31
	from *Diversions*:	
	No. 1	32
	No. 2	33
Paul Creston	from *Five Little Dances*:	
	Rustic Dance	34
	Languid Dance	36
Michael Valenti	*Prelude No. 4* (from *Piano Preludes*)	37
Gian Carlo Menotti	from *Amahl and the Night Visitors*:	
	Don't Cry, Mother Dear	38
	Have You Seen a Child?	40
George Antheil	*Little Shimmy*	42
	La Femme 100 Têtes, No. IX	43
Morton Gould	*Abby Variations*	44
Leonard Bernstein	*For Felicia Montealegre* (from *Four Anniversaries*)	53
Roy Harris	from *Little Suite*:	
	Sad News	56
	Children at Play	56
	Slumber	57
John Harbison	*Anniversary Waltz* (from *Four More Occasional Pieces*)	58
Norman Dello Joio	*1/3's* (from *Short Intervallic Etudes*)	60
Leon Kirchner	from *Little Suite*:	
	No. 1, *Prelude*	62
	No. 2, *Song*	64

UNDER THE WILLOW TREE
from the opera *Vanessa*

Samuel Barber
arranged by Henri Noel

to Noal
PEASE-PORRIDGE HOT
No. 1 from *Eight Piano Pieces*

David Diamond

Copyright © 1940 (renewed) by G. Schirmer, Inc. (ASCAP) New York, NY
International Copyright Secured. All Rights Reserved.
Warning: Unauthorized reproduction of this publication is
prohibited by Federal law and subject to criminal prosecution.

JUMPING JACKS
No. 2 from *Eight Piano Pieces*

David Diamond

Copyright © 1940 (renewed) by G. Schirmer, Inc. (ASCAP) New York, NY
International Copyright Secured. All Rights Reserved.
Warning: Unauthorized reproduction of this publication is
prohibited by Federal law and subject to criminal prosecution.

ROCK-A-BYE, BABY
No. 6 from *Eight Piano Pieces*

David Diamond

LULLABY
No. 8 from Eight Piano Pieces

David Diamond

TANGO
from *10 for Deborah*

Morton Gould

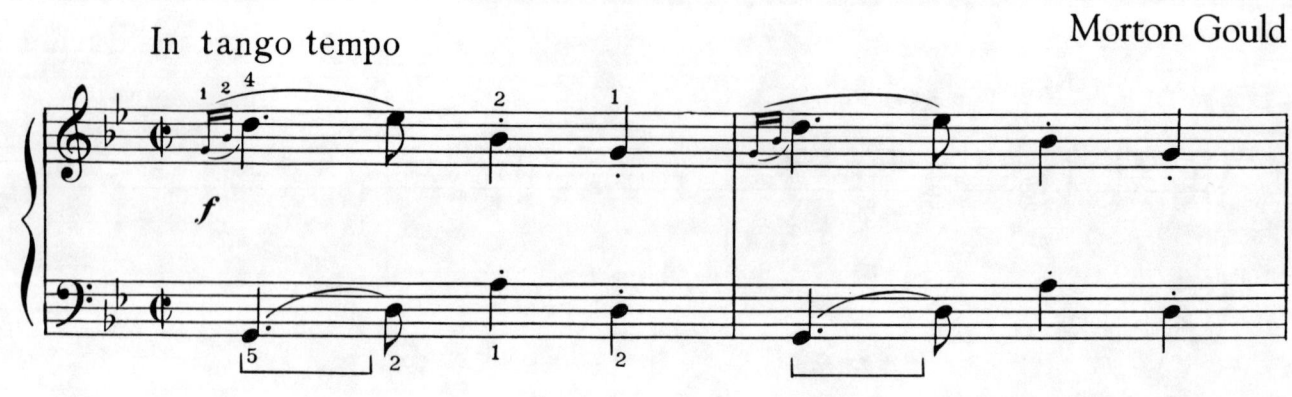
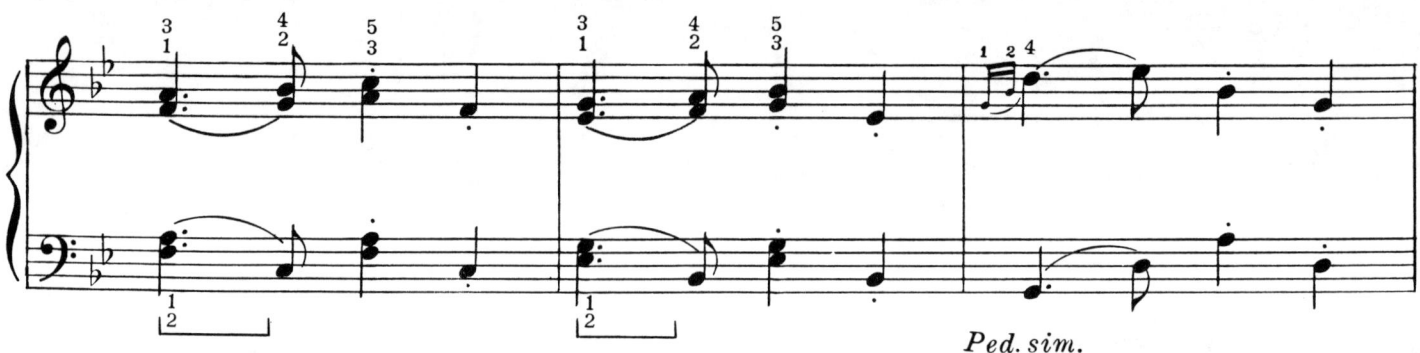

Copyright © 1965 (renewed) by G. Schirmer, Inc. (ASCAP) New York, NY
International Copyright Secured. All Rights Reserved.
Warning: Unauthorized reproduction of this publication is
prohibited by Federal law and subject to criminal prosecution.

WISTFUL
from *10 for Deborah*

Morton Gould

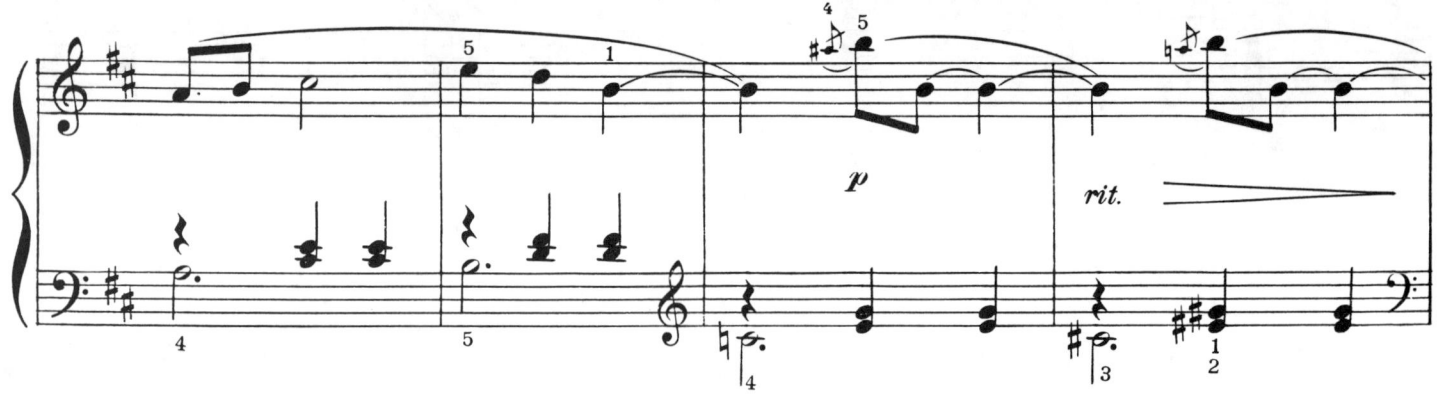

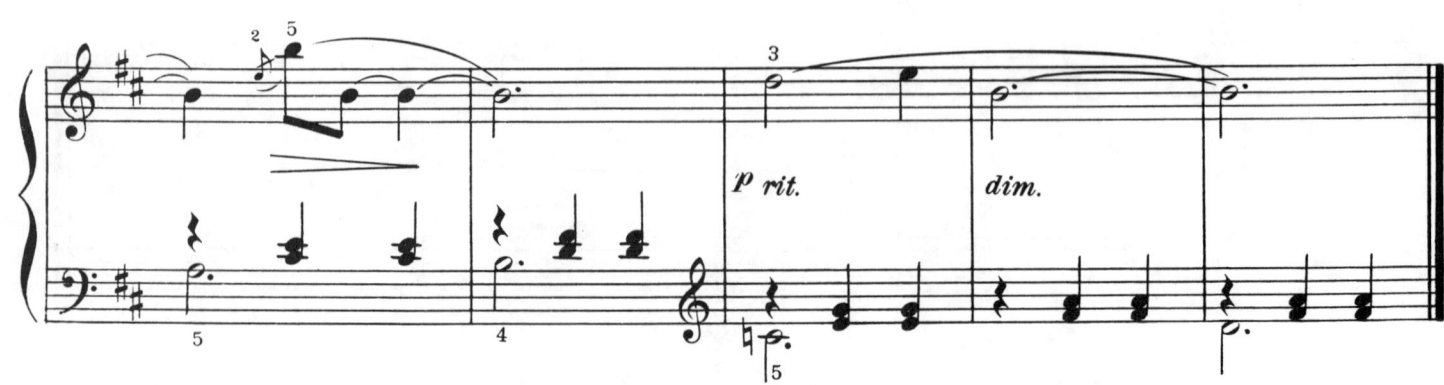

Copyright © 1965 (renewed) by G. Schirmer, Inc. (ASCAP) New York, NY
International Copyright Secured. All Rights Reserved.
**Warning: Unauthorized reproduction of this publication is
prohibited by Federal law and subject to criminal prosecution.**

DRIFTING
from *10 for Deborah*

Morton Gould

Copyright © 1965 (renewed) by G. Schirmer, Inc. (ASCAP) New York, NY
International Copyright Secured. All Rights Reserved.
Warning: Unauthorized reproduction of this publication is
prohibited by Federal law and subject to criminal prosecution.

LOUD AND SOFT
from *10 for Deborah*

Morton Gould

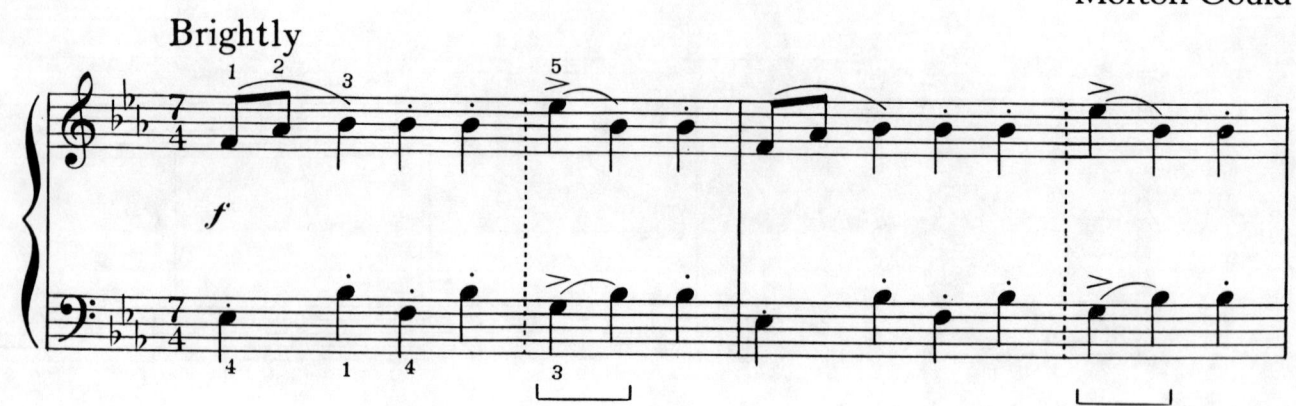

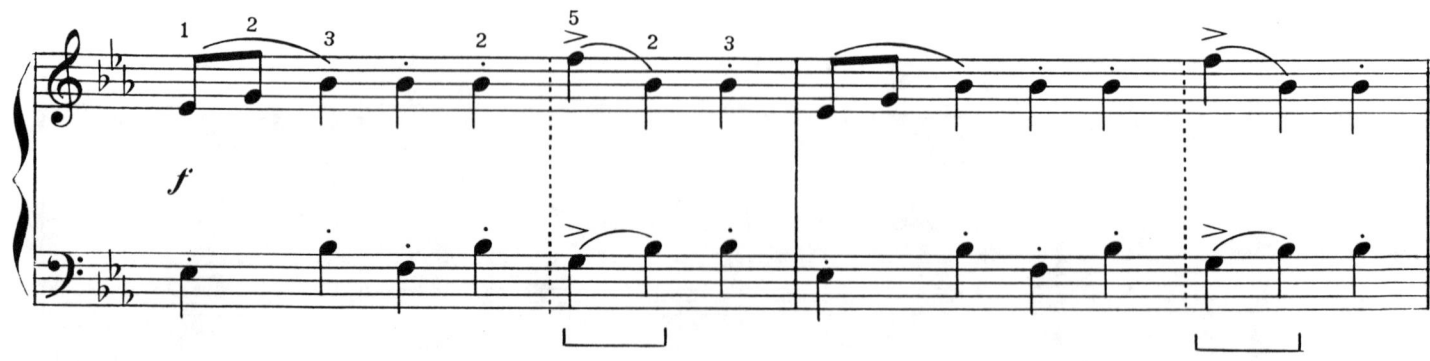

Copyright © 1965 (renewed) by G. Schirmer, Inc. (ASCAP) New York, NY
International Copyright Secured. All Rights Reserved.
**Warning: Unauthorized reproduction of this publication is
prohibited by Federal law and subject to criminal prosecution.**

MELODY
from *10 for Deborah*

Morton Gould

Copyright © 1965 (renewed) by G. Schirmer, Inc. (ASCAP) New York, NY
International Copyright Secured. All Rights Reserved.
Warning: Unauthorized reproduction of this publication is
prohibited by Federal law and subject to criminal prosecution.

A HAPPY ENDING
from *10 for Deborah*

Morton Gould

Bright and gay

Copyright © 1965 (renewed) by G. Schirmer, Inc. (ASCAP) New York, NY
International Copyright Secured. All Rights Reserved.
**Warning: Unauthorized reproduction of this publication is
prohibited by Federal law and subject to criminal prosecution.**

TO A WILD ROSE
from *Woodland Sketches*

Edward MacDowell, Op. 51

METAMORPHOSIS ONE

Philip Glass

Copyright © 1988 by Dunvagen Music Publishers, Inc. (ASCAP) New York, NY
International Copyright Secured. All Rights Reserved.
Warning: Unauthorized reproduction of this publication is
prohibited by Federal law and subject to criminal prosecution.

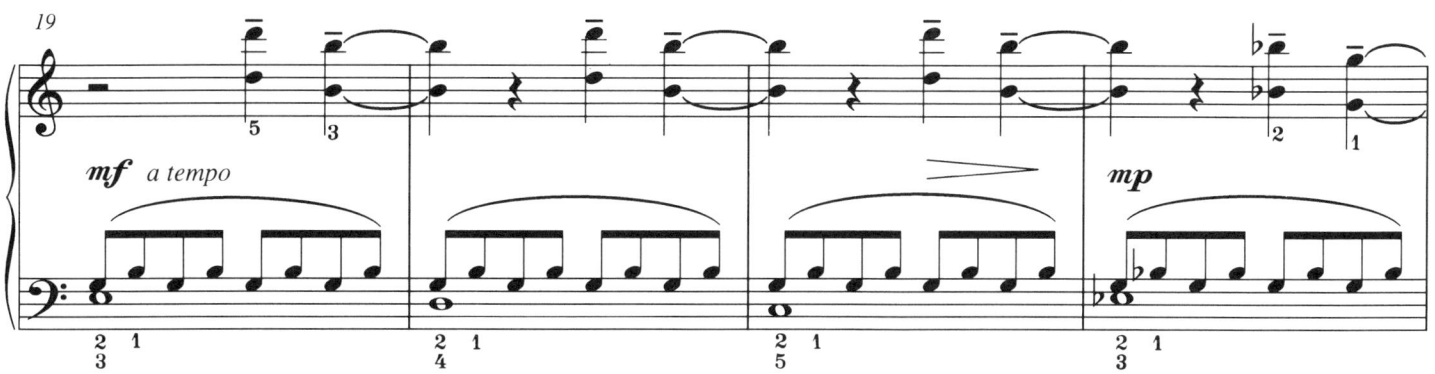
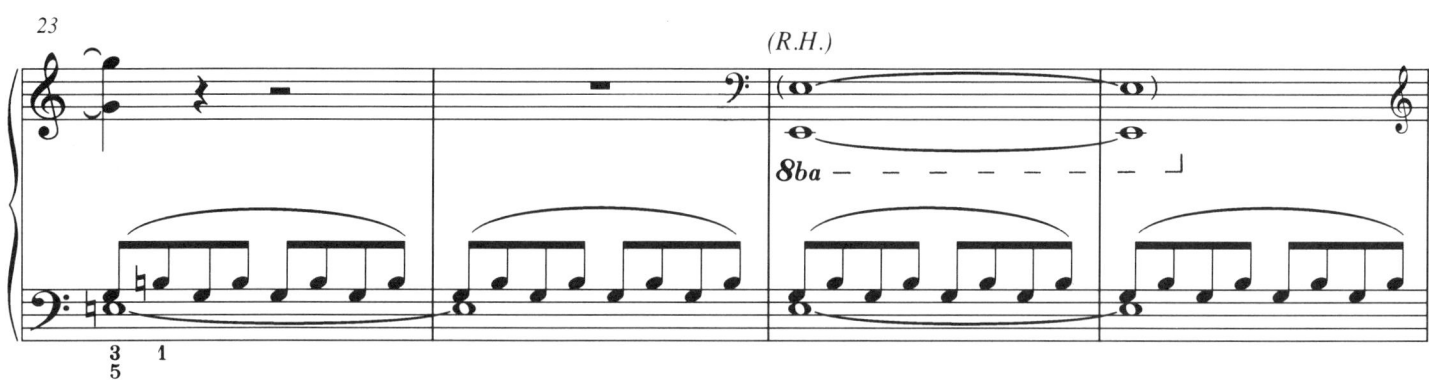

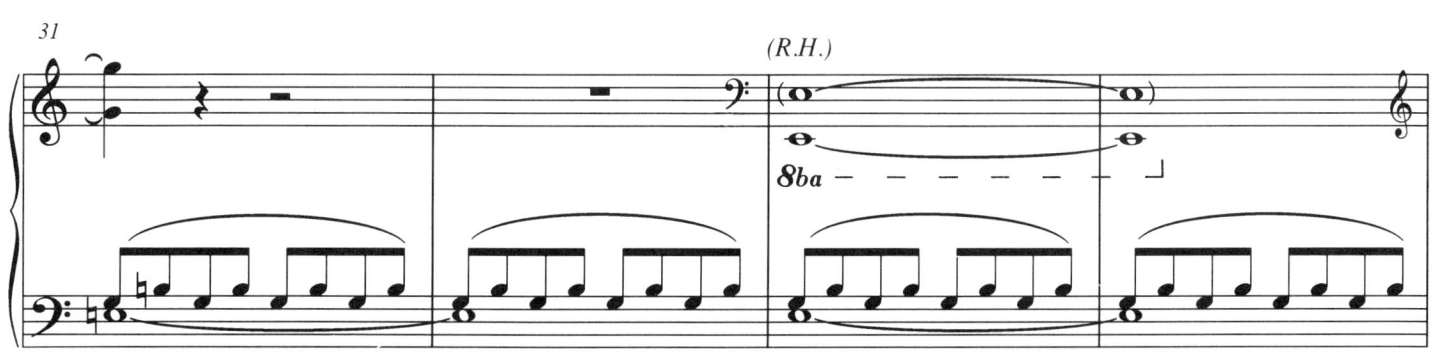

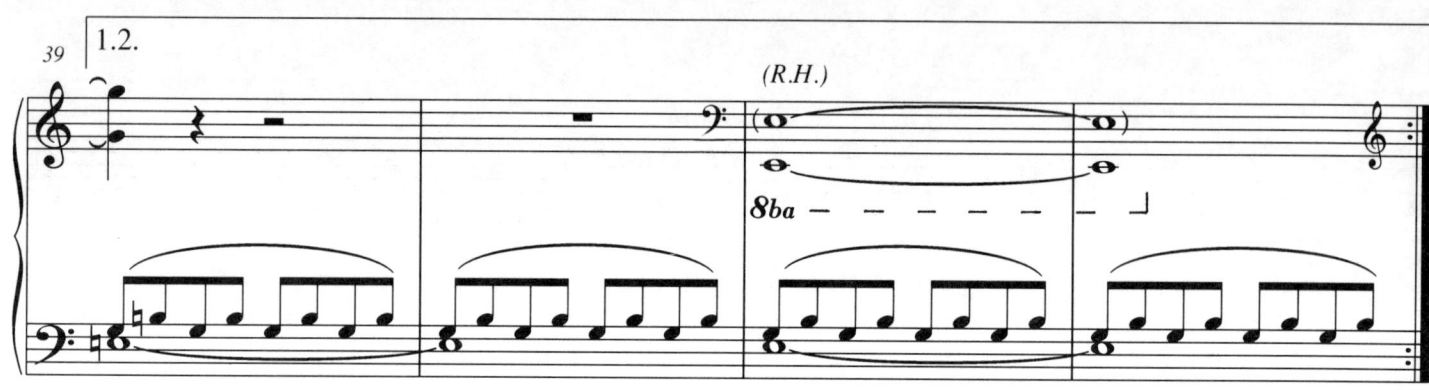
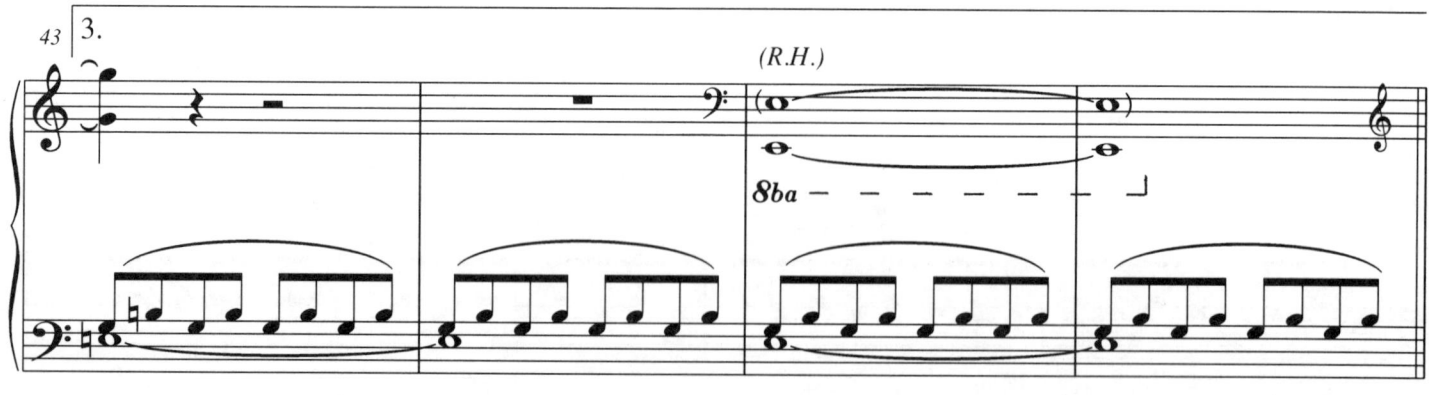

METAMORPHOSIS THREE

Philip Glass

28

FABLES
No. 1

Robert Muczynski, Op. 21

FABLES
No. 8

Robert Muczynski, Op. 21

FABLES
No. 9

Robert Muczynski, Op. 21

DIVERSIONS
No. 1

Robert Muczynski, Op. 23

Copyright © 1970 by G. Schirmer, Inc. (ASCAP) New York, NY
International Copyright Secured. All Rights Reserved.
Warning: Unauthorized reproduction of this publication is
prohibited by Federal law and subject to criminal prosecution.

DIVERSIONS
No. 2

Robert Muczynski, Op. 23

RUSTIC DANCE
from *Five Little Dances*

Paul Creston, Op. 24, No. 1

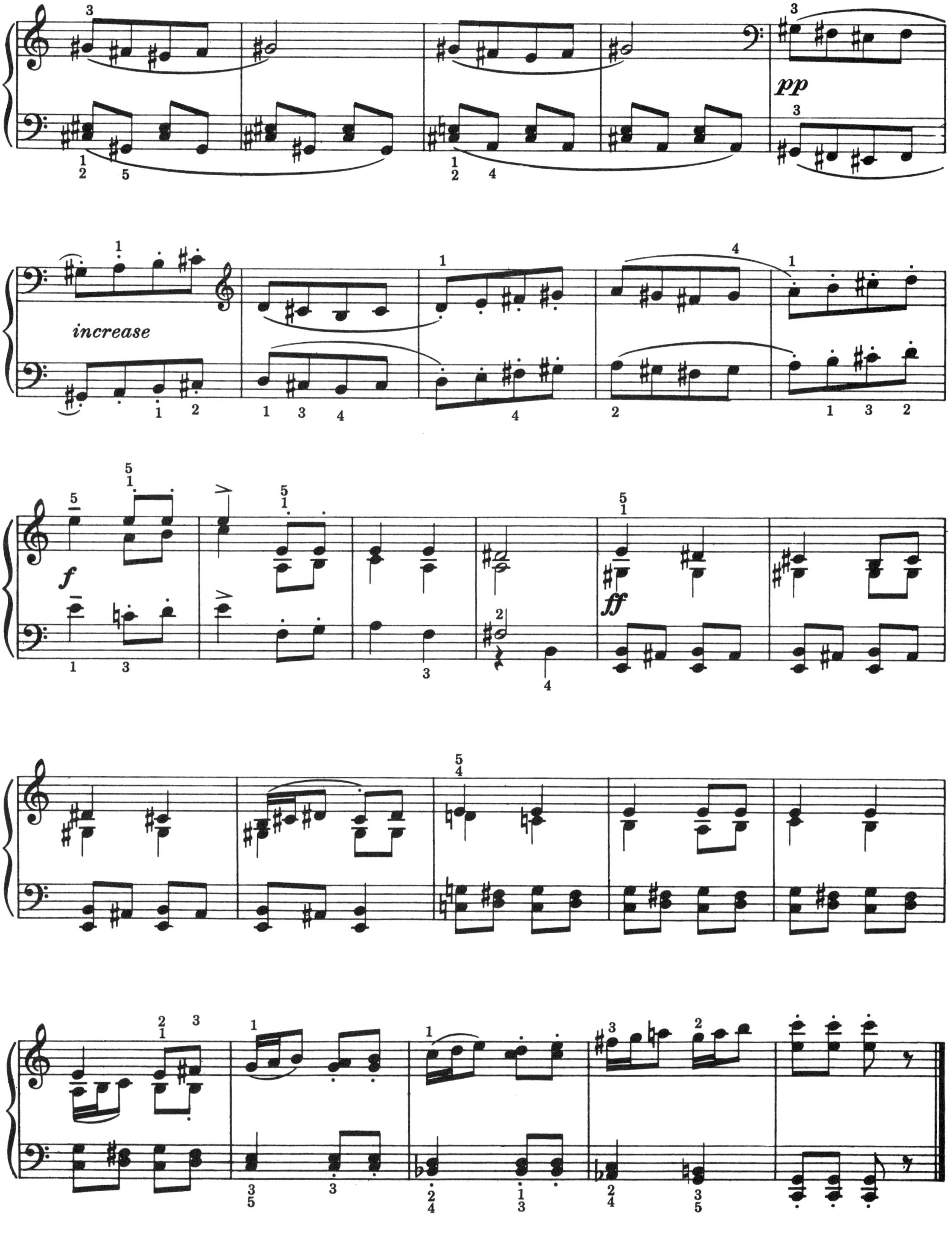
pp
increase
f
ff

LANGUID DANCE
from *Five Little Dances*

Paul Creston, Op. 24, No. 2

PRELUDE NO. 4
from *Piano Preludes*

Michael Valenti

DON'T CRY, MOTHER DEAR

from *Amahl and the Night Visitors*

Gian Carlo Menotti
arranged by Bill Boyd

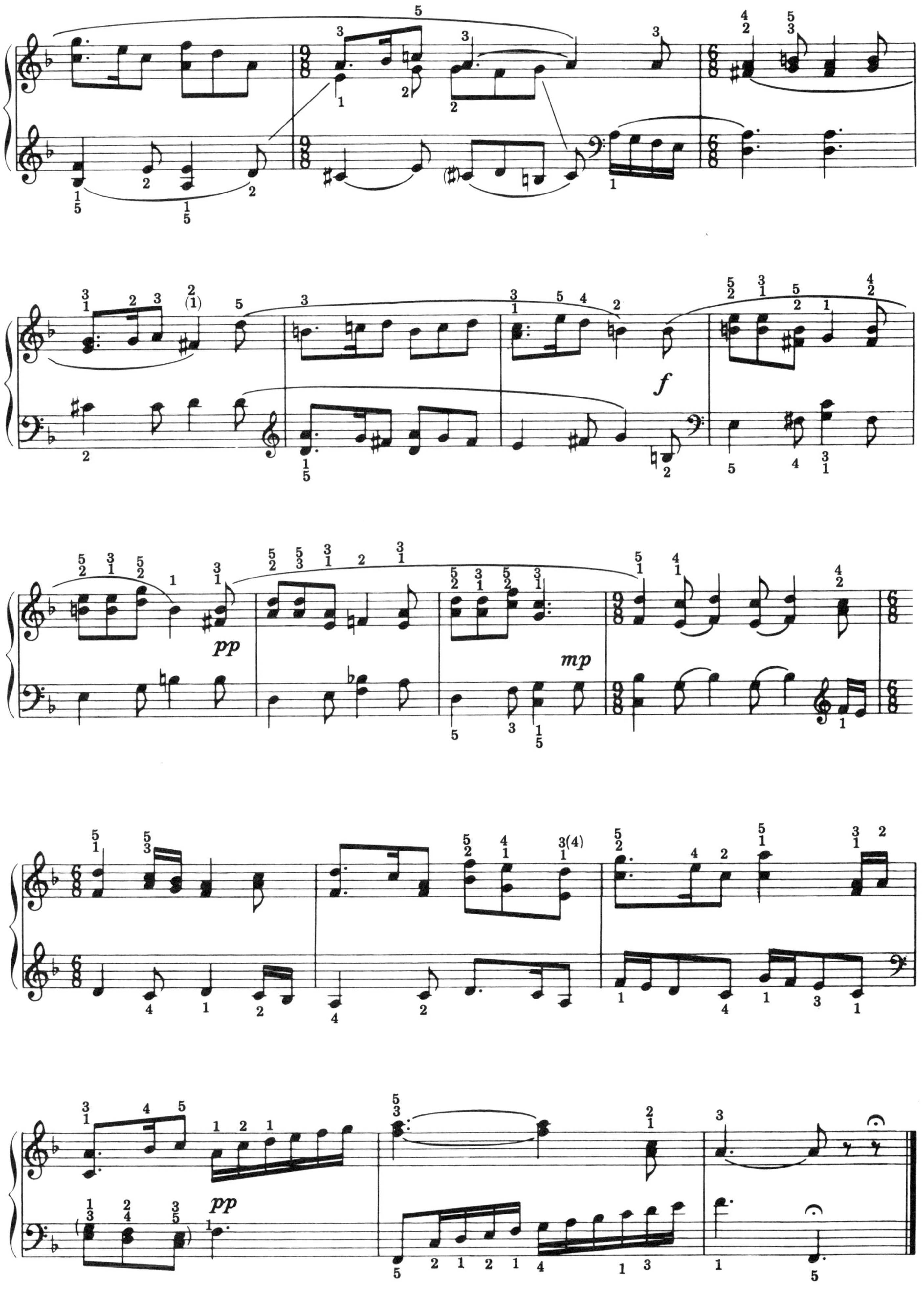
f
pp
mp
pp

HAVE YOU SEEN A CHILD?
from Amahl and the Night Visitors

Gian Carlo Menotti
arranged by Bill Boyd

Andante calmo, quasi adagio

41

für mein nur Einziger Böski

LITTLE SHIMMY

George Antheil
(1923)

LA FEMME 100 TÊTES
NO. IX

George Antheil
(1932 – 33)

ABBY VARIATIONS
Theme and 12 Variations for Piano

Morton Gould
edited by Joseph Prostakoff

45

Var. 4 — Moving easily

Stately, bell-like
Var. 5
ff
Keep pedal down to the end
p
cresc.
ff
ff
dim.
p
pp

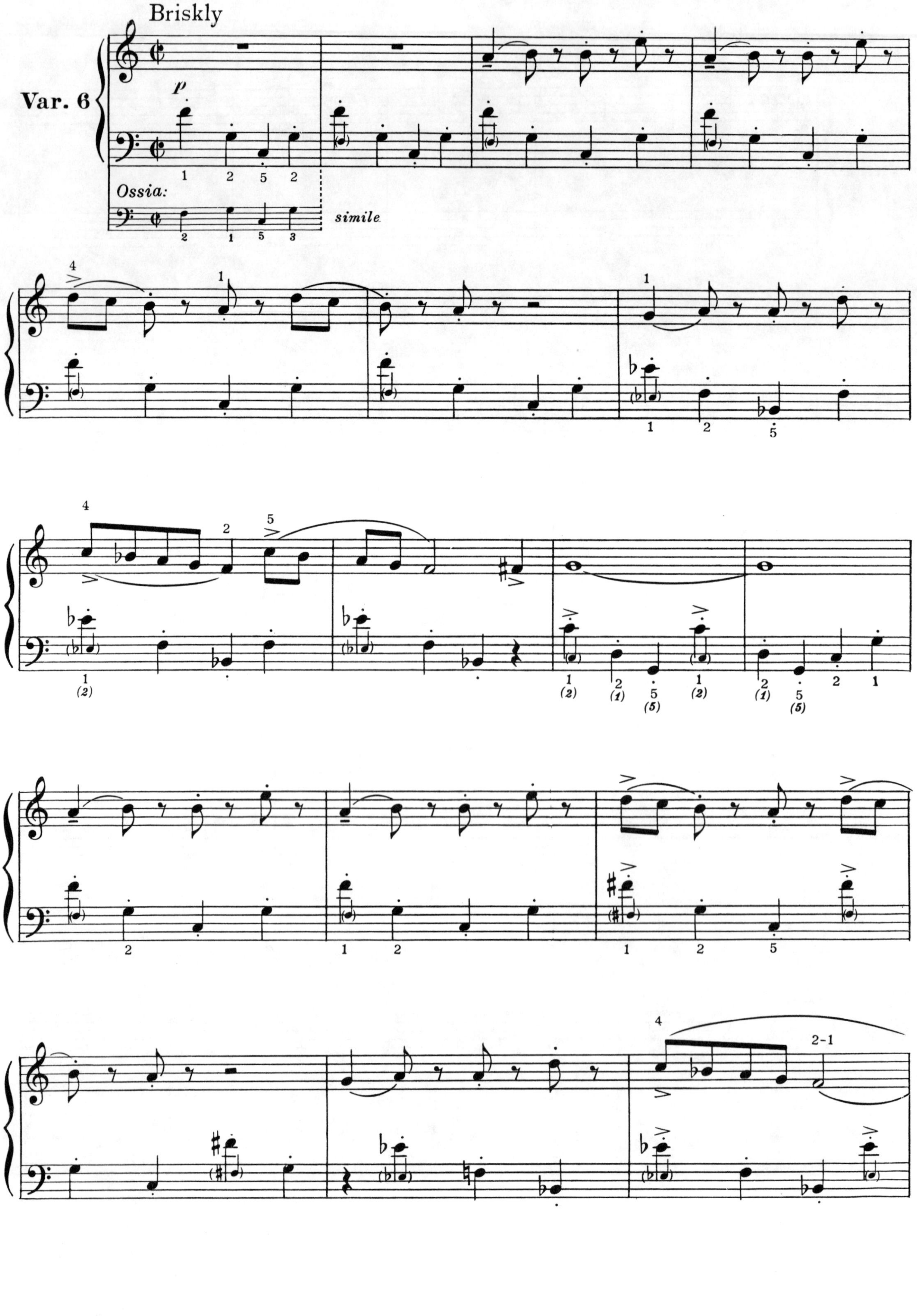
Briskly
Var. 6
p
Ossia:
simile

49

Very fast

Var. 8

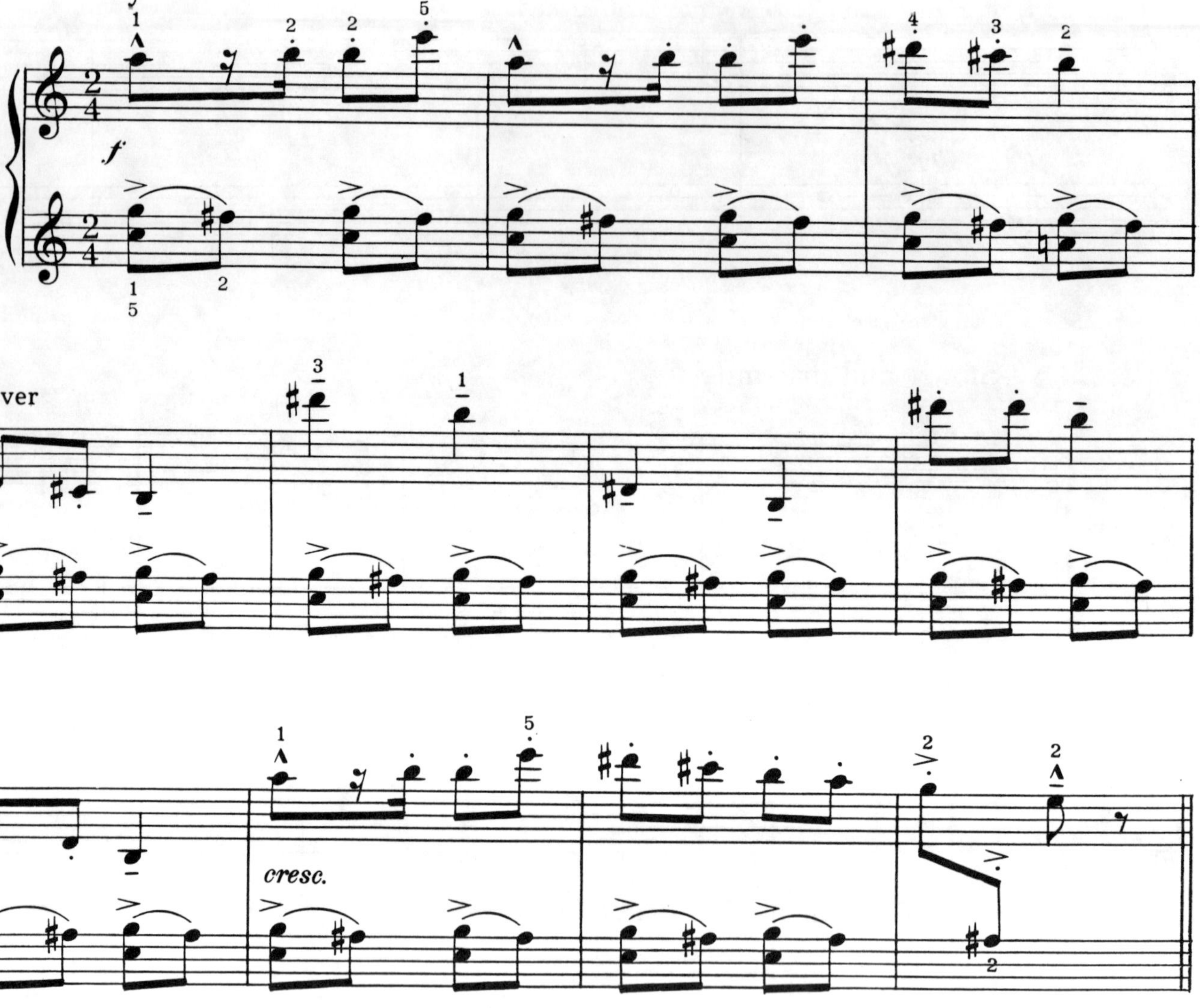

Fast and crisp

Var. 9

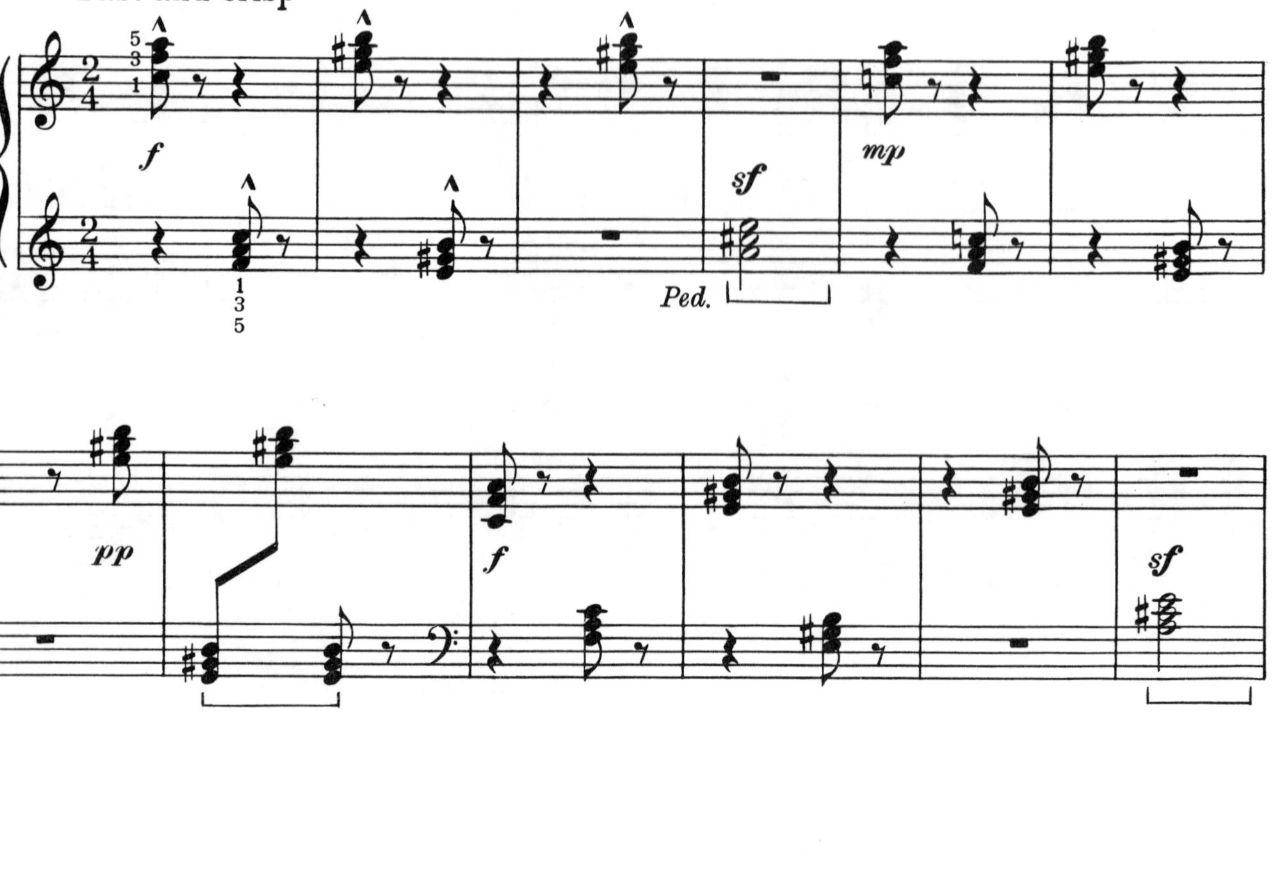

Slowly
Var. 10
p
pp
R.H.
L.H.
Ped.
pp
very gently
dim.
rit.
Moderate tempo
Var. 11
p short
f
mf
ff

52

Var. 12 — Happy and gay

FOR FELICIA MONTEALEGRE
from *Four Anniversaries*

February 6, 1922

Leonard Bernstein
(1948)

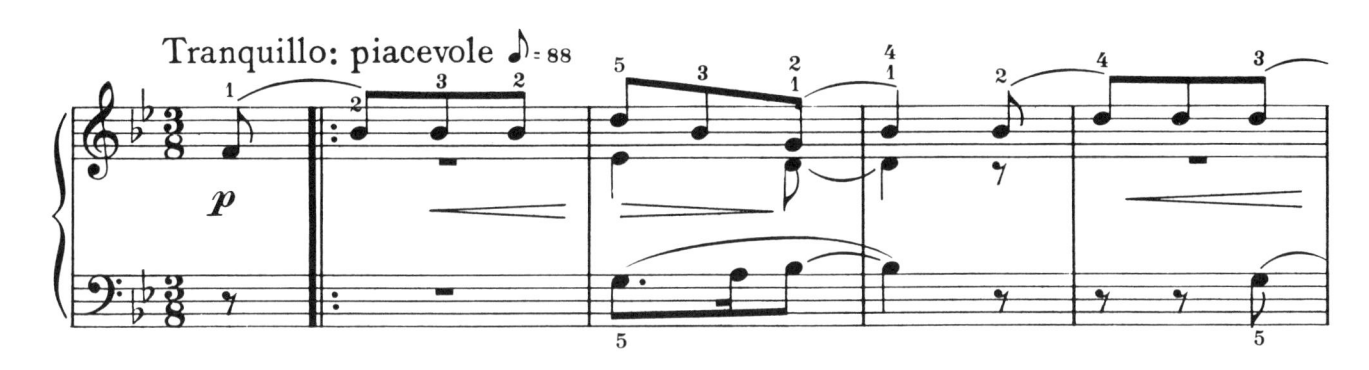

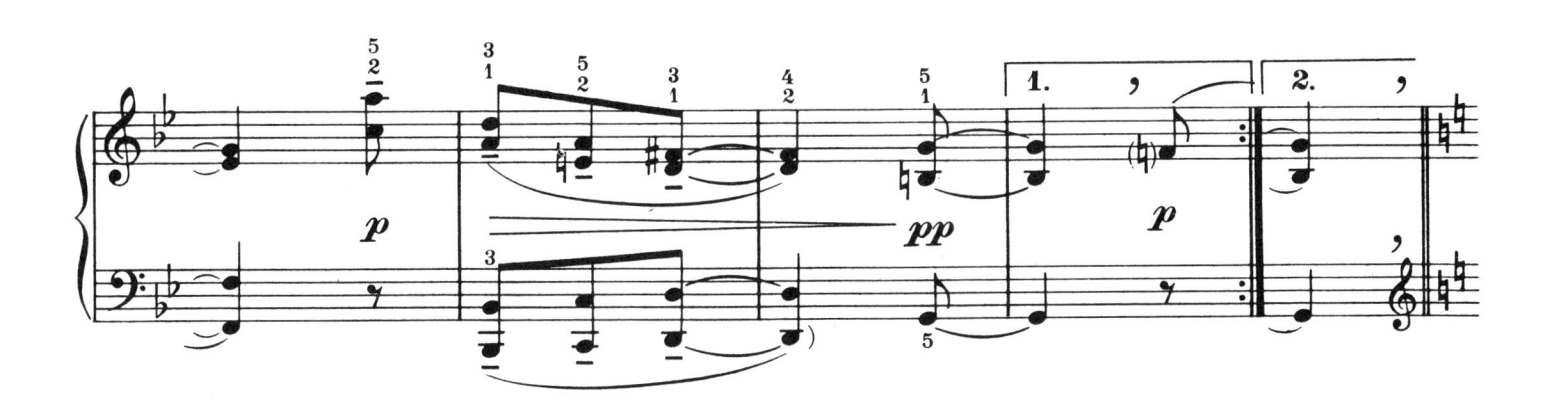

Pochiss. più mosso
pp legatissimo
sempre pp
cresc. poco a poco
mf
f
dim.
p
cant.

sensibile
cresc.
meno mosso
f
dim.
dolce
p, teneramente
più rit.
poco f, espr.
Lento
pp dolce
ppp

SAD NEWS
from *Little Suite*

Roy Harris

CHILDREN AT PLAY
from *Little Suite*

Roy Harris

SLUMBER
from *Little Suite*

Roy Harris

Copyright © 1939 by G. Schirmer, Inc. (ASCAP) New York, NY
International Copyright Secured. All Rights Reserved.
**Warning: Unauthorized reproduction of this publication is
prohibited by Federal law and subject to criminal prosecution.**

for Rosie Harbison

ANNIVERSARY WALTZ
from *Four More Occasional Pieces*

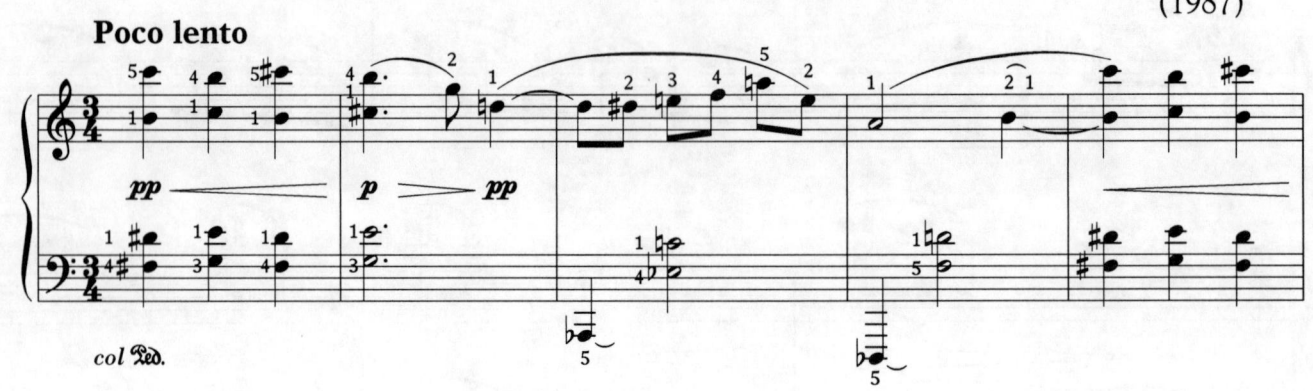

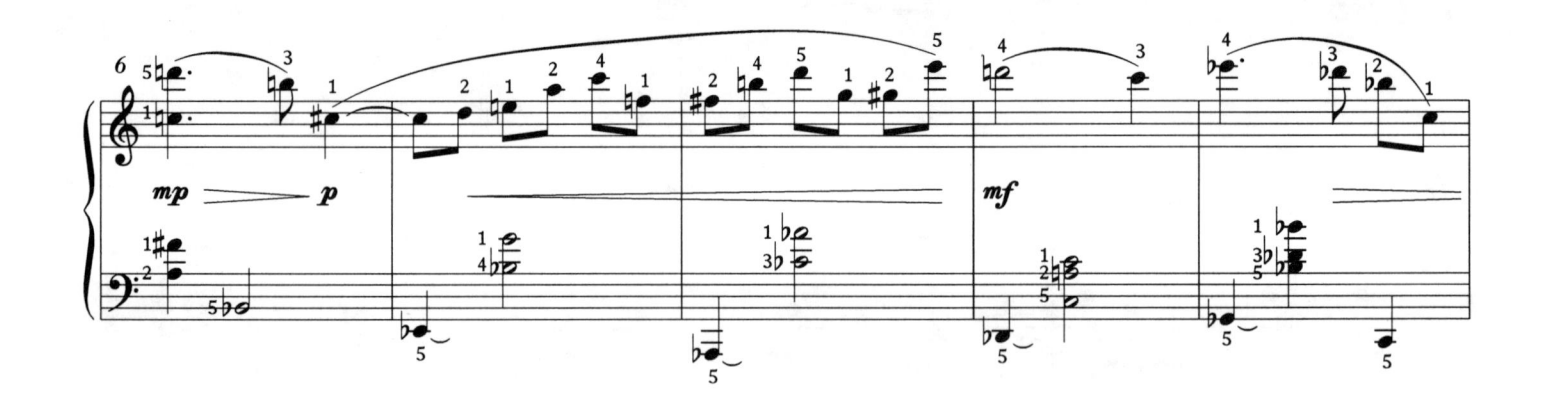

John Harbison
(1987)

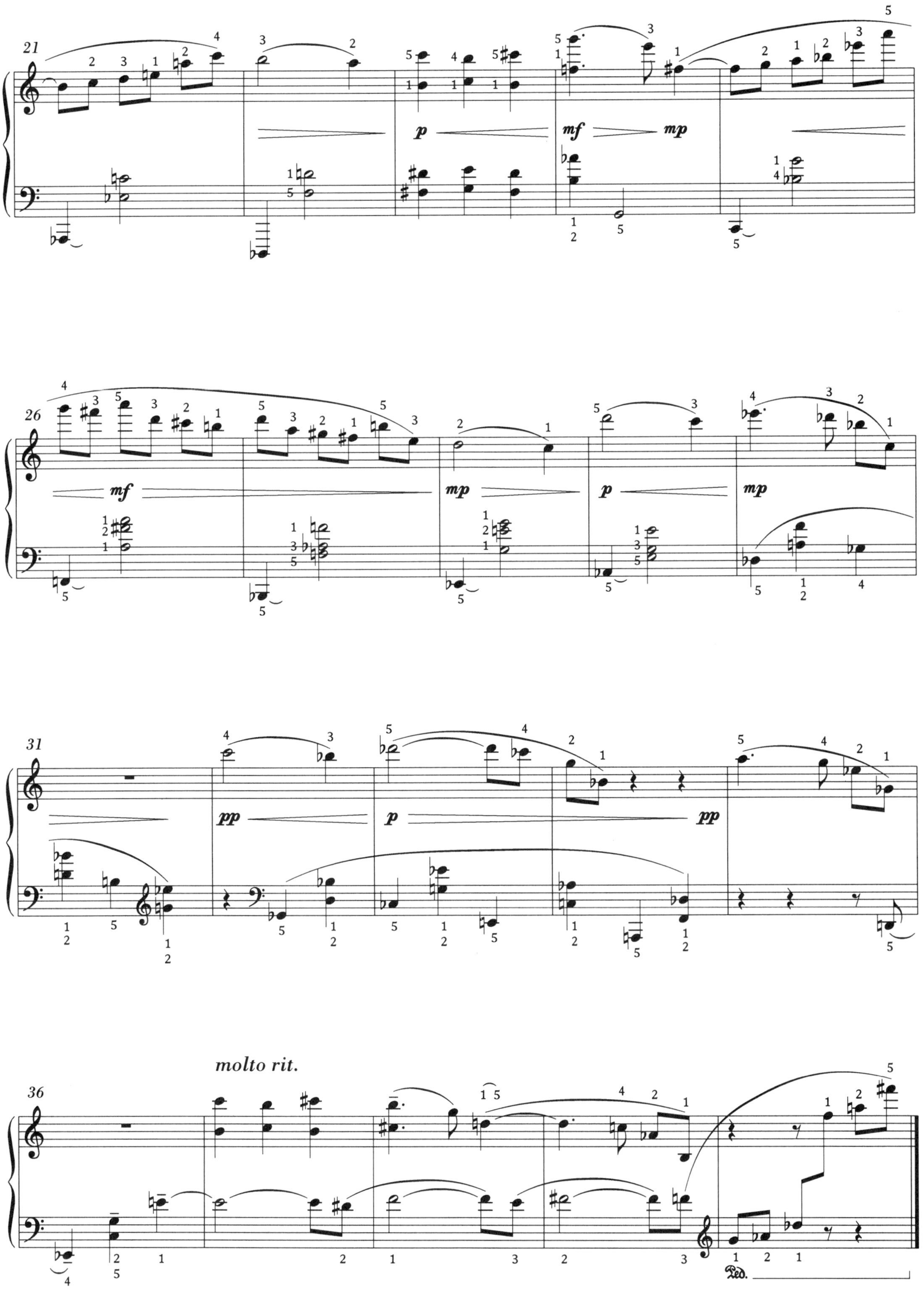
mf
mp
p
pp
molto rit.
Ped.

1/3'S
from *Short Intervallic Etudes*

Norman Dello Joio

61

for Gertrude
PRELUDE
No. 1 from *Little Suite*

Leon Kirchner

63

SONG
No. 2 from *Little Suite*

Leon Kirchner